PATCHY COASTAL FOG:
From Manhattan to (West) Marin in 24 Not-So-Easy Stages

PATCHY COASTAL FOG:
From Manhattan to (West) Marin in 24 Not-So-Easy Stages

by
Paki Stedwell

POINT
REYES P.O. BOX 332
PRESS POINT REYES, CA 94956

Typesetting and production by Hillside Setting
Cover design by David Bunnett

To the spirits of James Thurber, Charles Lamb and S.J. Perelman

AUTHOR'S NOTE

If you are reading this, may the cosmos bless and keep you! You are among the one-tenth of one percent of Americans who still read anything other than HBO listings and as such are very dear to a writer's heart.

If you enjoy the book that follows, could I ask you a favor? Tell one friend about it. Or two. If everyone who reads this book did that, POINT REYES PRESS might be in the black by the year 2000. Let's give *TV Guide* a run for its money, demonstrate that there are at least a few literate people left in this, the Dark Age of the non-genre printed word.

CONTENTS

PREFACE

This book is about being a Manhattanite let loose in the wilds of Marin. To Californians, Marin is hardly wilderness. But to an ex-New Yorker, some of the differences between Manhattan and West Marin require a lot of adjusting to. For example, one needs to have a very good relationship with the god of fire to stay warm in West Marin; in New York, all you had to do was pay the rent.

Another example of the difficulty of trans-coastal adjustment is that in West Marin, garbage is kept in cans, whereas in New York, it's used for sidewalk mulch.

The above are just two of the important and controversial differences between East and West coasts I'd like to explore in this book. As is customary with most Prefaces, I would here like to pay homage to the background of "Patchy Coastal Fog," which, by felicitous coincidence, is the same as the author's.

The sole by-product of the coupling of two radical, boisterously bohemian artists, I was born on the Lower East Side of Manhattan — in a Salvation Army hospital — the year World War II ended. (My birthplace probably has a lot to do with my fondness for thrift shops as well as tambourines.)

The Lower East Side of New York is a strange place for a person of the WASPish persuasion to be born. Mind, we were poor WASPs, *sans* the family connections, Tiffany pablum spoons, and Harvard degrees one usually associates with the stinging set. My mother and I moved all over the island of Manhattan, but no matter what the local neighborhood demographics (we went from the Lower East Side to Greenwich Village back to the Lower East Side and then to the Upper East Side), I was an outsider. I've since discovered that nearly every child experiences this feeling of being an alien, but in my case, no shit, it was *true*.

Which leads me back to my central point. Because I looked, talked, and thought so differently from my school peers (who were at first Italian Catholics and then lower middle-class European Jews), I was repeatedly asked if I was from California. This was comparable to being asked if I was from outer space, such is the average Easterner's conception of our State of grace. But now, firmly and probably forever a convert to the California way of life, I see that my peers were practicing kiddie clairvoyance, reading my future domicile like tea leaves in my aura. Now that I've been in California for more than ten years—and thus constitute a Native—I can only be grateful for having been pointed in the right direction.

P.S.
Inverness Ridge, 1983

ACKNOWLEDGEMENTS

Grateful acknowledgements to my family and friends for tolerating, even encouraging, the voluntary exile from Greenwich Village....

1 ADAPTATION: Cope Is Also a Four-Letter Word

New York is a universe unto itself; adapting to anything different, such as California, can be tricky since The City's laws of survival do not necessarily pertain anywhere else. For instance, due to the lack of crowds on West Marin streets, there's no one to shove out of the way.

When I left New York more than a decade ago, I felt like an ancient explorer, fairly certain that when I stepped off the island of Manhattan, I would fall off the edge of the world. Such is the New Yorker's narrow vision of the planet. Yet even though I now know there are places other than New York in which life is sustained, and that leaving Manhattan is not the same as leaving the universe, it was, for me, the same as leaving the *known* universe.

Even though I had a positive motivation for leaving New York—I knew there was a Better, Saner Way of Life Out There—there were some heavy adjustments to deal with. While I thought I was looking for a slower, more relaxed way to live, when I found it, all I did was fall asleep. Living at first in San Francisco and then the excessively rural Lake County, I suffered from Culture Shock, wherein I began to suspect there *was* none outside NYC. Then came Energy Warp, in which I felt as though I was running on 220 volts while everyone around me was running on candle power.

The next phase of adjustment was Integration, when I tried to change some of my spots and merge with my new landscape. I haven't done too well with the very last phase—Camouflage—but I'm still learning. (A New Yorker's spots are hard to hide.)

Having met many other ex-New Yorkers since my voluntary exile, I've been able to make a few generalized observations about how some of us handle the ordeal of becoming *exes*. Some return to New York once a month to recharge their will to live; others disdain the city for years, preferring not to remind themselves of what they're missing. Still others, the best-adjusted, return when they feel like it and don't miss New York at all. These are the same types of people who don't mind the idea of dying or paying taxes.

Adjustment to the loss of New York can be a painful, grief-

1

stricken process—where else can you get those soft, warm, chewy pretzels they sell on the streets? But, in time, the popovers at the Station House come to surpass the yearned-for New York food. The only thing missing is the crunch of the street grit. In West Marin, the bakeries try to duplicate this experience by using poppy seeds. While it's a very hip attempt at substitution, it serves to point up some of a New Yorker's difficulties in adapting to the California mode. I mean, street grit is bad for you, it makes you tough, puts mean in your muscle. What do poppy seeds do, aside from get stuck between your teeth?

2 ANTIDOTES TO HOMESICKNESS: What I Think About When I Start Missing New York

Nostalgia for New York doesn't happen very often, but when it does occur, there are a few choice scenarios I dwell on to make the homesickness go away. The major ones are:

1) Wearing brand-new, expensive city duds as it suddenly starts to rain while other New Yorkers pole-vault over me trying to catch a cab. There is no phone nearby, no bus shelter, all the stores on the block are closed, and there's a bunch of scuzzos across the street eyeing me as thoughtfully as if they were doctors and I was a tax write-off.

2) Having a bladder or bowel attack while I'm on a crosstown bus in rush hour with a driver who's brake-happy. A woman with a screaming infant is on my right and an old man with numerous bulky packages is on my left — which he alternately drops in my lap or sticks in my eye. Then, as he begins to have an epileptic seizure, he becomes convinced I'm the ghost of his late wife.

3) Going to the new "in" spot and being denied entrance because I don't look like the right stuff. Going next door and finding I can't get it there, either; they also only take people with the name *Women's Wear Daily* tattooed on the inside of their upper lip.

4) Looking for an apartment.

5) Realizing that even though I can make oodles of money in Manhattan, half of it goes to the shrink I need to stay sane while the other half goes for taxis.

6) Being marooned on a city street corner in January, waiting for a bus that never comes, so I can get to a job I don't want, while the only thing between my legs and a wind-chill factor of − 20 degrees F. is a pair of Ultra Sheer pantyhose.

It's hard for New Yorkers to be humble when their street performers are usually better than divas in Dallas.

3 ATTITUDES:
A Very Important Person

Partly to compensate for the crush of other people around them, all New Yorkers, from bankers to bag ladies, adopt the attitude of being Important. When in New York, it's wise for one's aura to exude the impression that one is a Very Busy, Very Important Person Whose Agent is Waiting at Elaine's to Consummate a Very Big, Very Important Deal.

(I used to hang out at Elaine's *before* it was world-famous. Does that make me Important, Pre-Important, or someone who missed the boat?) If one's aura does *not* advertise the afore-mentioned importance, one is steamrollered faster than one can get indigestion from a potato knish.

Imagine my chagrin, then, when I hit West Marin and discovered that all my training in being Important was obsolete. Antediluvian, even. So I set about re-designing my aura to match that of my new community. I'm not quite finished yet, but Total Laidbackness is almost within my grasp. The only trouble is, I sense the wind of change blowing through the attitudes of West Marinites in the 80's. Am I crazy, or do I see more and more people scurrying around, looking busy, acting preoccupied and in general appearing to be on the brink of being Important? That's okay with me—after all, I have all that valuable previous experience to fall back on—I just have one question before I meet my agent. We have to decide which West Marin spot is the local Elaine's—Manka's or the Two Ball Inn.... Please, it's important!

Leaving New York is a golden opportunity to start one's own zoo. The main thing to keep in mind with animals, however, is that when sick, they don't always respond to infusions of chicken soup.

4 CITY SKILLS/COUNTRY SKILLS: Never the Twain Shall Meet

Adapting to life in the country, for an ex-New Yorker, means giving up certain cherished city skills and trying to learn their country counterparts. For instance, one of the most valuable tricks I ever learned in New York was how to get a seat on the subway at rush hour. This is a talent I intend to pass on to my progeny, for a price, but it pains me to realize it's not as important, in West Marin, as lighting a good fire—something that still fills me with apprehension and nervousness. Fires see me coming; I am sure the kindling talks to the newspaper and says nasty, derogatory things like, "She couldn't get a can of Sterno going." Whereupon they raise their internal kindling point and become immune to my matches, pleas and tears.

My love-mate used to be quietly amused at this woeful lack of country smarts on my part; now he laughs out loud. I feel called upon to point out several things. Firstly, that he was raised in the Mark Trail tradition in the back woods of Massachusetts and Vermont. While he was sharpening his survival skills, I was honing mine, on the whetstone of urban guerillahood. To return to the subway analogy—not only would he be unable to get a seat at rush hour, he would most likely be mangled trying to get through the turnstile.

Another area of great differentiation between its city and country versions is that of pedal perambulation: walking. My love-mate alternates between the Nature's Way shuffle and the Gait of Power, while keeping a sharp eye out for wildlife, fungi, and other points of country interest. This mode of transportation would be fatal in New York, indelibly marking him as a Tourist. There are people who hang around street corners in New York City with the sole purpose of ogling obvious non-New Yorkers, hooting inside metropolitan jokes at them and making fun of their Bass Weejuns.

Another contrast: I hate to hike and consider it a crime against nature, but I do know how to do the New York walk. The Big A is one of the few places on earth where it's conceivable to be arrested for walking under the legal speed limit, which, last time I was there, clocked out at about 17 miles per hour. In addition to speed, in order to correctly perform this conceit of the concrete, there are certain other rules of form that must be observed. The first is the arms-at-the-side holding pattern. In New York, this is so pickpockets can't get into your pants or "pockabook." But outside New York, it looks as though one has just mortared one's armpits.

Another attribute of the New York walk, while I'm on the subject, is a sort of slight hunching over of the head, neck, and shoulders, giving most city-dwellers a vague resemblance to turkey buzzards. This stance has obvious protective properties in New York—it helps shield the body's vital organs from frontal attack. But if I practice my old way of walking in West Marin, I'm quite likely to be taken for a winner in a turkey buzzard look-alike contest.

The most time-consuming aspect of walking around New York—avoiding eye contact—is another way in which a basic skill such as walking changes from East to West. Out here, not looking around at the boundless natural beauty would be considered unnatural; in New York, the only things to look at are a million other pairs of eyes, many of them belonging to deranged persons. And so one learns not to look too many people in the eye, for all New Yorkers know that to look madness in the eye is to risk catching it.

To sum up, breaking into the boonies for an ex-New Yorker can be trying, but then I remind myself that life in The City was not always restful. In general, I'd have to say that even at its worst, country life is no more nervous-making than a gang of junkies following me into my building.

I thoroughly deplore my lack of country skills but then I come from a place where a challenging home improvement project was putting up a new toilet paper holder. People in West Marin are somewhat daunting against this background, with their penchant for tossing up houses, barns, and garages. But my city smarts haven't totally deserted me. Since the idea of long, hard years learning how to survive in the woods didn't tickle my fancy, I did the next best thing—by shacking up with someone who already knew.

8

5 CLOTHING/FASHION: From Bergdorf's to L. L. Bean

As part of the transformation from East to West Coaster, I notice that I buy more and more clothes from L. L. Bean each year. Even in the relative wilds of West Marin, one must conform to the local dress codes.

People in New York dress like they're going to the opera just to catch a bus, saving their rags to wear at home. It took me a long time to catch on to the fact that it works the other way around in my new neighborhood; people wear their good clothes at home and dress *down* when they go out. I still haven't determined if this is due to a reverse ethic of shab as chic or if people in West Marin secretly practice clothing abuse. In any case, for someone who used to care about what was in or out, West Marin can be a fashion vacuum. Unless, that is, one adopts L. L. Bean as the country version of Mr. Blackwell's Best Dressed List. The only trouble with Bean's stuff is that it never wears out, so you're stuck with it Forever, which is very practical but terminally boring.

I still have a problem with over-dressing, though, frequently fooled into thinking that a party is an occasion for dressing up. (Old habits die hard.) But in West Marin, a call for a party only means putting on a clean tee-shirt, wearing your least-holy jeans, and buffing up one's Birkenstocks. Maybe eventually I'll learn it doesn't mean skirt, dress, or real shoes.

Of course the other problem with trying to follow fashion in West Marin is our mean, sometimes positively nasty, temperature. When you need several layers of clothing just to stay warm and dry, color coordination goes out the window. I mean, who cares if your river driver's shirt matches your fisherman's sweater or not?

New York makes one paranoid about the way one dresses; there's a very big magazine there that has a monthly feature of the backs of terribly dressed people — pointing out what's wrong with their outfits, their figures, their shoes, etc. I never wanted to see myself immortalized on that page and so spent much time making sure my slip never showed. It is lovely to be without the superficiality of that kind of thinking, but don't people out here like the idea of personal adornment at all? (And I'm not talking new sweat suits, either.) What if we instituted an Annual West Marin Black & White Ball? No, forget it, I'm getting carried away again; the only ones who'd come would be the social-climbing clique of our cow population.

Another thing I miss about East Coast fashion was occasionally wearing something *flimsy*—like a negligee. I brought one or two with me when I moved out here, but they've long since mildewed from non-use. With the thermostat set on (sigh-of-the-times) LOW, my main association with little wisps of undergarments is no longer SEX, but COLD. My idea of a good time in bed since I've moved to West Marin is wearing a new set of thermal underwear.

The one thing you couldn't get away with wearing in New York, in polite society at least, was polyester anything. Californians in general are much more tolerant of synthetic fabrics—except natives of West Marin, whose motto is, "If it's not natural, it's not nice." The local version of polyester is animal skins, environmentalists being the big guns in town. I've even been warned what would happen to my family and certain cherished shrubs if I wore my grandmother's ancient racoon coat on Main Street.

So I return to the safety of jeans and Bean's. It seems ironic that whereas jeans started out as a fashion protest by nonconformists, they have now become the uniform of the masses. I still love my denims, but wonder occasionally if we could get Bean's to manufacture the Perfect West Marin Outfit, which would consist of a thermal-lined, denim-patterned wet suit, with coordinating flippers cut out to look like Birkenstocks. The crowning *piece de resistance* would be the obligatory West Marin hand-crocheted beanie. It would look, as my mother likes to say, "Neat, but not gaudy," and would establish Pt. Reyes Nation firmly on the fashion map—right up there with Pocatello, Paducah, and Podunk—as a hotbed of *haute couture*.

6 CRIME & OTHER DANGERS: It Isn't All in the Streets

As a smart ex-New Yorker, that is, one who survived the city's sizeable contingent of robbers, muggers, and rapists, I always more or less assumed that I would have it made anywhere else. I mean, I was a graduate with honors of big-city assault avoidance and couldn't see how my sixth sense about street crime—which meant not being in the wrong place at the wrong time—would desert me when I left NYC.

But I wasn't counting on West Marin, scene of such pastoral beauty that one is lulled into a sense of false security. Slowly but surely, the old New York rules of conduct started slipping away. I stopped hiding my money in my bra, threw out the miniature can of Mace on my keychain, and even became trusting enough to stop keeping armed guard over my clothes in the laundromat. Eventually I even renounced the New York norm of seventeen locks on my front door.

Just when my guard was almost completely down, I realized who the real potential villain in my new locale was: Nature. In the city, just for a reference point, a natural disaster is defined as missing the weekly visit from the exterminator. And so once again, my New York background made me vulnerable; I saw trees as oversized houseplants rather than three stories of uncut lumber that could pulverize me. Rain, in New York, was often a pain but it never, as in recent West Marin flood years, threatened one's very life and home. And the sun, when it was out, was either a curse (in summer), or a blessing (in winter), but never, as in Northern California's drought, something that sucked up one's water supply while death from dehydration loomed.

It seems supremely ironic that one should have to live on a hair-trigger of alertness even in the country, but since that appears to be the case, for survival's sake I've retooled my city training and taught myself to think of Mother Nature as the neighborhood street gang, out to get us ex-New Yorkers when we least expect it.

11

So far, I haven't found the Northern California counterparts of three living NYC landmarks: Moondog, the black baglady with the surgical mask on 34th Street, and the guy on roller skates with the umbrella hat—but then they're probably in L. A.

7 ENTERTAINMENT: Which Way to Broadway?

New Yorkers are snobs about a lot of things, and entertainment's one of them. Against the backdrop of Lincoln Center, Madison Square Garden, and Carnegie Hall, finding entertainment in West Marin was quite a challenge. Even our local, laudable Dance Palace can't be expected to take the place of the Great White Way and so, after a study of some of the native forms of entertainment—trying to find what you want at Building Supply, watching the barber's pole revolve in front of Earl's, and throwing wine-and-cheese-tasting benefits for endangered sub-species of newts—I cast about for other likely substitutes and settled on the closest to home: our flora and fauna.

I found, in time, that the plant and animal world can supply all the stimulation of New York *kultur*, if one simply readjusts one's perspective. For instance, in terms of dramatic action, there are few books or movies more engrossing than the minute-to-minute struggle to protect my outdoor plants from the ravages of our multitude of predators. Next comes the pivotal plot point for a morality play: to kill or not to kill.

For natural forms of art and sculpture, there's Elephant Mountain as well as Bishop pines. The music of the spheres is supplied by our songbirds, wind, and ocean's roar. (Exceptions are the Stellar jays and screech owls, who take the place of atonal punk bands.)

For comedy, there are hummingbirds. Due to the way the little jeweled beauties dive-bomb each other whenever we put out their feeder, we've named their antics the Hummer Wars since it's obvious they've seen too many George Lucas movies.

And for horror, there are slugs. Two items of natural history of which I was blissfully unaware while growing up in New York were 1) the number, and 2) the *size* of the West Marin banana slug. Whereas I've adjusted to sharing my turf with this slimy mollusk, I realize how far I've come from my city sensibilities when I reflect that just the sight of one of these ten-inch-long creatures would put most New Yorkers in a pine box.

As you can see from the above, I don't have much time to miss opera, late-night clubs or the theater. I've seen the likes of Barbra Streisand and even Katherine Hepburn on Broadway, and while they were brilliant, I've replaced them with the thrill of seeing other types of rare and exotic birds, such as a pileated woodpecker. My backyard is a natural floor show and besides, I hear we're supposed to get cable TV next year.

8 ESSENTIAL SERVICES:
Learning to Go Without

New Yorkers come to expect all manner of services at any hour of the day or night. There aren't too many other places in the world where you can get cleaners, florists, and especially food and liquor stores, to deliver at three in the morning. Not having to leave your apartment for anything is probably the best thing about living in New York.

Giving up these life-support systems was another painful adjustment for me. It took a long time to accept the fact that I no longer had 24-hour access to such essential emporiums as drugstores, pizza parlors and Häagen Dazs dispensaries. The most crippling deprivation was the lack of any local Smiler's, a New York chain of delicatessens whose specialty is catering to the millions of nocturnal bulimics in the city, or people whose preferred pig-out periods are between midnight and dawn. Of course, now that I live in the wantonly healthy West Marin, I wouldn't dream of having those late-night cravings for a meatball hero, washed down by a quart of cream soda, followed by half a gallon of Breyer's peach ice cream, but this habituation has not come easily. For the first couple of years out of New York, I stocked a larder that would have fed Moby Dick; now I practice the bypass technique of going to bed early.

Another essential service for most New Yorkers—all-night locksmiths—cater to the large group of the just-burglarized. This is not as urgent a need outside NYC, but I did find myself panicking once or twice when I found I could not add to my collection of locks at the drop of a hat. Until, that is, I solved the problem by going country, getting a bear trap and setting it just inside my door.

Some of the other frustrations of an ex-New Yorker living in West Marin include being deprived of a quick fix at the neighborhood shoemaker's, which dot the city like welcome little pit stops. I used to love the leather-and-shoe-polish smell of those little cubbyholes, and the chance to sit down in the middle of an otherwise-frenetic day. Out here, getting your shoes re-soled is a major goddam expedition and usually includes being without them for weeks at a time. There are only two solutions that I can think of: enslave your own little Italian cobbler or develop a bare foot fetish.

The most essential service in New York is performed by the keepers of the sane: psychiatrists. Although they're often much maligned, having a good shrink in the city can mean the difference between browsing through Bloomie's and taking intravenous at Bellevue. In West Marin, problems tend to be less severe and I find I can achieve almost the same results I used to get lying on my back spewing forth by having a good, long ride on my horse. The latter costs about as much as the former, but I don't begrudge the expense; my horse is a hell of a lot cuter than my former shrink and, so far at least, he hasn't asked me if I suffer from penis envy.

FOOD:

9 A Jug of Calistoga Water, a Loaf of Seven-Grain, High-Fiber Bread, and One's Significant Other

In my circuitous route to West Marin from Manhattan, I first had to pass through several other localities. Being a person who likes to eat, I naturally made some observations about the differences of eating and dining customs between East and West coasts, as well as points in between.

The first and most traumatic of these differences are the ones pertaining to that most delectable of New York food for the soul — pizza. As the years wear on and I am unable to find any local version that even comes close to the gorgeously gooey satisfactions of my hometown, I have, sadly, come to the conclusion that ex-New Yorkers don't die of old age or natural causes, we die of R. P. D. (real pizza deprivation).

Many foods changed names once I left the bright lights of NYC. Scallions turned into green onions; seltzer, or two cents plain, turned into club soda; most importantly, I learned not to order a hero sandwich, fearful that the local American Legionnaires might have me arrested for fast-food cannibalism.

While passing — as quickly as possible — through the Midwest, I mistook a small bowl full of water on a restaurant's table for a fingerbowl. The waitress looked aghast when I stuck my fingers in it, informing me that it was, in fact, the way they drowned flies. I think it was after eating in this same memorable restaurant that I concluded that in many American small towns, *haute cuisine* really means the Jack-in-the-Box Supreme sandwich.

I gradually became wary of restaurants that featured a blinking neon sign outside; their best fare tended to be olives, onions, and lemon twists. I also grew chary of any eating establishment that boasted "New York-style" food, having to be painfully reminded that Buffalo was a part of New York and that that was what they were talking about.

While I have been able to find many New York food favorites since I left — one can even get matzoh in West Marin — it has been difficult to say goodbye forever to prune lekva (a heavenly whipped prune jam). An event comparable to the Second Coming will occur when any store in West Marin begins carrying Fox's U-Bet Syrup; almost comparable to the joy of this event will be the day health food stores stop trying to pass hummus off as edible.

One of the more puzzling things about Northern California restaurants (and this definitely includes San Francisco and West Marin) is their lack of atmosphere. I've been told that Chinese restaurants eschew any kind of interesting decor because they believe it would detract from customers' concentration on the food; what's the non-Oriental restaurants' excuse? They certainly can't claim a shortage of interior decorators.

The *biggest* difference between eating out in New York and the West Coast is the absence of any Mexican restaurants in New York and the invasion of them out here. I was a bit nonplussed at what used to be scores of Chez Charles' turning into dozens of Casa Carlos', but I think I've figured out the reason New Yorkers are resistant to the Tex-Mex explosion—there are simply too many people who have to live too close together.

Growing up in New York means growing up half-Jewish; no matter what one's ethnic origins, it's impossible to ignore the influence of the dominant culture around you. Thus, I thought Sundays were created for the consumption of bagels, lox, and cream cheese and that apple pie was the obsolete term for apple strudel. After traumatizing the entire family of a Jewish girlfriend by asking for milk with dinner—they were serving pot roast—I learned not to mix dairy with meat. What I'm saying is that one adjusts to the local customs, no matter how bizarre. So I'm hopeful that in time I'll stop dreaming about coffee breaks at Chock Full O' Nuts and come to tolerate, if not love, herb tea and tofu doughnuts.

10 FRIENDS & RELATIVES: Leaving Old, Making New

Leaving some relatives, particularly my then-in-laws, was an important motivating factor for getting out of New York. When told of our impending move, certain relations-by-marriage (they know who they are) tried every trick in the book to keep us from leaving: "Are you prepared to accept charity if you can't find work?"

When that didn't work, they tried guilt trips: "How can you do this to us?" Next came sly jabs at our sanity: "Leave New York — for California? Don't you know only out-patients live there?"

Friends were a whole other ballgame. It was painful to watch old friendships dwindle as the months and years went by and we didn't return to the Big Knish, but the sad fact was that no matter how hard we tried, we became outsiders, immune to the city's charms and thus, by extension, those of our friends. This process can be devastating to one's faith in immutable relationships, but it does have one overriding benefit: new friends become as precious as roses in January.

Modes of friendship change outside New York. Whereas in the city, one tends to have dense-pack friendships — a tight group of people with whom one cruises around — out here I've noticed that relationships, like the geography, are more spread out, less ingrown. In general, I know lots more people in West Marin than I ever did in New York, but we see each other less often. This is because, contrary to the Great California Myth, everybody's so busy scrambling after a living. Either that, or my deodorant is defective.

Especially right after leaving the city, I tended to gravitate toward other ex-New Yorkers as the only people who could understand my deep, unfulfilled need for challah bread and real egg creams. Also, only other ex-New Yorkers could empathize with the fact that living in New York was like living on the verge of orgasm — thrilling but debilitating.

After almost ten years in West Marin, I'm just starting to feel settled and secure with my non-New Yorker friends. I doubt if I'm in the running for the Most Mellow Award, but at least I've given up letting out Bronx cheers and yelling "Taxi!" at parties. Instead, I

19

say positive things about everything, count the threads in my natural fiber clothes and boast about how much bran I've eaten that day, just like everybody else.

11 THE GREAT OUTDOORS: Is It Really Good for You?

Like many New Yorkers, I used to have one basic problem relating to nature: I was allergic to it. And I mean mentally as well as physically. Years of living in concrete canyons took their toll by depriving me of my natural senses. I was acclimatized to air pollution, but couldn't seem to adjust to clouds of pollen.

When I first got to West Marin, I tended to view unfettered nature with a slight alarm; it was too vast, overpowering, unknown. My New York background had taught me that the only people who looked up at the sky were those who had just been mugged and were lying down to rest.

I had to completely re-think my relationship to the environment. In the city, this consists of looking out the window to see what to wear. Turning on the faucet is the closest city-dwellers get to the natural elements that support life, but outside NYC, one becomes aware that having enough water to run a bath is a gift from the heavens, not something that comes with the lease.

I had much to learn. To wit, that trees are individual, noble entities — not canine pee poles. Also that, in the wild, flowers don't grow mixed with baby's breath. Some of my surprises weren't always pleasant. I discovered that the country has its own form of noise pollution: birds.

Now when I take a trail ride on my horse, and I can SEE the vast and incredible beauty of my new neighborhood without having an anxiety attack and BREATHE the wondrously fresh air without choking, I realize how far I've come from my New York days, when trekking through the wilderness meant, honestly, taking a cab through Central Park.

God made Sundays for yardwork and/or worship, not necessarily for staying in bed trying to get through the Times.

12 HOBBIES: What Are They?

New Yorkers don't allow themselves leisure time so dealing with non-work hours was a nasty problem for me after I left the city. My love-mate has a penchant for moving things, preferably bushes and trees he had planted in the wrong place the first time around. While this seems to satisfy him, it doesn't quite do it for me. Part of me's still stuck in the New York groove of either wanting to work, party, or sleep; it's been difficult for me to accept the fact that in the rest of the world, there are things called *hobbies* which were designed for pure and utterly useless *personal pleasure*. This is a basically shocking concept for an ex-New Yorker, imbued as I am with the city's credo that one is either Successful or, the only other option, Worthless. The more time one devoted to hobbies, according to the New York way of thinking, the closer one got to becoming Worthless because it would mean time detracted from the effort of becoming Successful.

Besides, I knew all too well that leisure activities could lead, like marijuana to heroin, to the sinfully hedonistic idea that all of life should be treated as a hobby, to wit, that it can be personally, perennially pleasurable. I prescribed a strict regimen of abstinence, at least until hobbies could be taken in moderation, without any attendant guilt or self-loathing.

I looked around at the hobbies of my West Marin neighbors, hoping to find something that I, too, could waste time on. Spying on Cal-Trans, measuring the amount of acid in our fog and writing long letters about the world condition to the *Point Reyes Light* just didn't get me heated up, probably because they weren't *useless* enough. Then I met a certain handsome, dark bay horse and have been, happily, taken for a ride ever since.

The process of hobby-hunting took a while; I call it Californiazation, wherein one sheds most of one's fears about excessive pleasure and slowly sinks into the hot tub of hedonism. Now that I'm up to my neck in it—my particular off-hours obsession evolved as dressage (the art of classical riding), otherwise known as the Sport of Kingsize Masochists—I can see, however, that the East Coast's warnings about hobbies were true. I do seem to crave ever-increasing amounts and it gets more expensive every year.

JFK is New York's revenge on anyone attempting to escape; SFO is the Bay Area's punishment for people attempting to emigrate.

13 INCOME: Why It Never Catches Up With Outgo

One of the bitterest pills to swallow about leaving NYC was that while money does seem to go twice as far outside the city, this gain is severely offset by the fact that one can only earn half as much.

I thought, naively, that leaving New York would enable me to beat—forever and with a big stick—the high cost of living, but I soon realized that living was ruinously expensive everywhere else, too, especially without my inflated New York income to compensate. For those who like to collect meaningless data, I offer below a list of items I thought I would save money on, and why these savings never materialized:

Taxis: These are a major item in any New Yorker's budget, costing anywhere from $50–$300 a week. In New York, the expense is worth it and can be likened to life insurance because while you're sitting in a cab you can't be getting knifed in a subway. Outside the city, though, instead of vanishing altogether, this budget item goes for paying one's personal taxicab, i.e., loan payments, gas tank locks, hubcaps, and fuzzy dice.

Entertainment: There are few nightclubs and even fewer Broadway theaters to deflate one's wallet in West Marin, but then again, when you have to drive twenty miles each way to see a movie, the savings in this area are negligible.

Food & Liquor: Everybody knows that eating costs more in West Marin than over the hill; the last time I grocery-shopped in New York, I found the prices about the same as at our own food stores, which is to say outrageous. The only place I've found that makes West Marin prices seem cheap is Maui. That, however, is not sufficient reason to go to a place where the best food to be found is a Wahini Whopper.

Vacations: Since few environments will drive one crazier than New York, I find I have been able to save a lot of what I used to spend on Fire Island or Hampton get-aways. The trouble with West Marin is that while it's so beautiful one doesn't need to go away as often as if, for example, one lived in Rohnert Park, reverse hydro-therapy in the winter does get costly.

For the uninitiated, elements of reverse hydro-therapy include: buying and then lying under a bank of sun lamps, repeating the mantra, Mazatlan, O Mazatlan; incessant daydreaming about seeing the sun again when one is supposed to be working, i.e., income-producing; inordinate consumption of various expensive euphoric drugs and alcohol; cost of extra house-cleaning help due to increased family food fights; and loss of bill-paying income due to purchase of more escapist books, records, and sex toys.

Rent: As bad as this was in New York, mortgage payments in West Marin are not exactly a steal, either.

Clothing: As previously noted, L. L. Bean stuff is generally cheaper than buying at Bloomingdale's, and one doesn't need quite the diversity of clothing that one does in New York, but for the winter months in West Marin, wardrobes made of rubber don't, as they say, grow on trees.

And so, in a nutshell, one doesn't save squat by leaving New York. One also has to be flexible about one's work. Since coming to California, I've discovered a strong entrepreneurial streak in myself. I've put on flea markets, rock concerts, and free-lanced—anything to keep from working for someone else. Since I'm a writer and, ipso facto, make about enough money at my craft to keep me generously supplied with paper clips, I saw three basic choices for supplementing my income.

One was to forge a trust fund and knock off a rich relative. Unfortunately, I don't have any rich relatives.

The second option was to take any kind of job, no matter how ill-suited or how much I loathed it, work as long as I could stand it, and then blow my brains out. This is not only a mortal sin, but messy.

The third, and only palatable alternative, was to start a cottage industry. I take things so literally that that's exactly what I do now—industriously rent out cottages. I haven't come close to earning my New York income yet, but I find solace in the fact that due to the relative lack of stress with my job, I'll undoubtedly live at least several weeks longer than if I were still in New York.

14 NEW YORKER QUIZ: Test Yourself

Question:

What do New Yorkers call people who leave the city to find an easier way of life?

What is one of the dirtiest words in New York?

What ends just past the boundaries of Greater New York?

How can you tell a visitor from a real New Yorker?

What do New Yorkers lose if they leave New York?

What's the biggest challenge of living in New York?

What's the real name of a rubber ball?

What's a New Yorker's advice for someone having a heart attack on a busy street?

Answer:

Hedonistic weaklings.

California.

The world.

The visitor's the one who turns around at the sound of someone screaming.

First their identities, then their minds.

Folding the *New York Times* while hanging from a strap on a crowded bus.

A Spaldeen.

Ignore it. Maybe it'll go away.

Walking is not practiced very much in California cities and so it's best, after leaving New York, to say goodbye to one's leg muscles, after assuring them you'll meet again in another life.

15 NEW YORK NOSTALGIA: Things Not to Think About

As in any good love-hate relationship, mine with New York is not all hate. There are many things about the city I miss occasionally, and even some I try not to dwell on too often as they can induce a bad case of Super-Saver blues. (Definition: when one can't even afford a quick trip back on the red-eye special.) Below is a list of some of the more evocative of these nostalgic no-no's:

• The tidal wave of palpable kinetic energy that carries one along just walking the streets of New York.
• Central Park after the first snow of winter.
• Brunch, drinks, or just loitering at the Plaza.
• Washington Square Arch at sunset on a balmy summer's night.
• St. Anthony's Feast in Little Italy.
• An opening night on Broadway.
• A half-off sale at Saks Fifth.
• A new exhibit at the Met.
• Chicken Kiev at the Russian Tea Room; veal scallopine at Sardi's; pasta con pesto at Elaine's.
• A leisurely stroll past the shops and art galleries of Upper Madison Avenue.
• Taking a cab down Park Avenue at night around Christmas.
• Lilac Chocolates!

Then, when my eyes stop watering, I harden my sensibilities, take a cold, objective look at my list of lovely memories and the *truth* about these nostalgic scenarios emerges.

• Tidal waves of energy can turn individuals in NYC into so many pieces of flotsam and jetsam being carried along on the swelling tide of noxious, over-crowded humanity.
• The beauty of Central Park after the first snow lasts about 3½ minutes before it becomes a depressing city park covered in freezing gray slush.
• Last time I was there, the Plaza Hotel was catering to a naugahyde salesmen's convention from Kansas City.
• Washington Square is hard to disparage, unless one has an unnatural aversion to socializing with junkies or having one's head

fertilized by pigeon droppings.

• St. Anthony's Feast is great fun; I just can't take all those baby goldfish in tennis-ball size glass bowls that will end up belly-up in two days.

• Opening nights on Broadway are now occasions for which one has to hock one's heirlooms to afford tickets.

• As for Saks, what kind of false, materialistic value system is at work in wanting to look exquisitely, fashionably dressed? (And anyway, one would be ostracized off the streets of West Marin for the crime of ostentation.)

• New exhibits at the Met, and even the old ones, are an un-abashed delight; the only trouble comes from feeling creatively humbled—or quashed, depending on one's mood—in the face of such mastery of the arts.

• The real hey-days of the Russian Tea Room, Sardi's, and Elaine's are over. It's true that a lot of their main customers are still name-droppers and dropped names, but who really wants to spend $43 per person, not including wine, just so you can say you sat in the same room with Bess Myerson?

• The main thing one will come away with after a stroll along Upper Madison Avenue is a feeling of severe financial deprivation.

• A cab ride down Park Avenue at Christmas *can* be heaven, especially if you find a cab before dying of hypothermia.

• Lilac chocolates are truly memorable. Unfortunately, so are the zits it causes.

Over the decade I've been gone, my nostalgia for New York has lessened appreciably, particularly when I study the above list. The only thing I can't bring myself to do is forego various New York rags, such as the *New York Times Book Review*, the *New Yorker*, and the *Village Voice*. I keep telling myself that the city's umbilical cord doesn't stretch as far as Inverness Ridge, but then the cost of a few magazines is a small price to pay for the illusion that I'm still In Touch.

16 PROS & CONS OF BECOMING AN EX-NEW YORKER: A Balance Sheet

The single best reason for becoming an ex-New Yorker is to avoid the daily demoralization of stooping over in the gutter to pick up one's dog's doodah. Mornings and late afternoons, the streets of the city are full of sophisticated, *soignee* New Yorkers doing their best not to look embarrassed as they spread newspapers, waft toilet paper, or produce poopscoops to whisk away the waste of their canines. But they can't quite hide their chagrin as streams of cars, trucks, and pedestrian passers-by give them the once-over to make sure they're doing it right. While K. P. (Kaka Patrol) is an essential ritual in the city, it ranks high on the list of why I congratulate myself for not being a New Yorker anymore. More degradation I don't need.

On the con side, to balance things out, one of the things I do miss about New York is political tolerance. There is a tacit agreement among New Yorkers not to get too worked up about other people's politics. This is undoubtedly because so many different races, creeds, and colors have to live like wombmates. Everyone may not like it, but intolerance of neighbors — or their politics — one meets every day at the garbage chute is not good for one's blood pressure.

By contrast, since I've been in California, I've seen many shared fencelines turn into Maginot lines as neighbors advertised for their opposing candidates. Even out here in mellow West Marin, one had best be prepared to defend oneself unless voting for the Good Guy, whose initials are also G. G. While I am basically a political mole (that is, someone who prefers to live in the dark but who occasionally bumps into a grass-root movement), my New York education taught me that whereas politics in the city is a rough and dirty game, it changes to just plain crazy, and plainly intolerant, everywhere else.

New Yorkers are justly famous for their political and especially religious tolerance, but sports are another thing entirely. One had to be very careful not to seat a Yankee fan next to a follower of the Dodgers at dinner parties in my home town or bread would not be the only thing to be broken together. Thank God I'm not in New York anymore; now all I have to remember at parties is not to invite parents of kids who are on opposing West Marin Youth Soccer League teams.

For the first couple of years out of New York, I counted my blessings that I would never have to see the city's mascot, the cockroach, again. I don't know why this admirably adaptive insect gives my flesh the crawls; I've tried many different types of therapy to try to lose my revulsion, but I still have a nightmare in which bands of marauding roaches swarm down my street singing "We Shall Overcome." Just about the time I thought I'd escaped one of the more harrowing trials of living in New York — cohabiting with cockroaches — I discovered its West Coast kissing cousin: the earwig. While they are equally creepy in my book, the main difference between the two (and believe me, I'm grateful) is that whereas the cockroach wants to cozy up to you and your food, the earwig at least keeps its distance and only takes the outdoors as its domain. To quote a famous New York saying: "So take it already, wear it in good health!"

A definite con about leaving New York is the reaction one tends to get from non-New Yorkers. For instance, when I first got to California (with my then-husband and baby), I settled in a small town in Lake County. Just because we bought an old Victorian church and wanted to turn it into a restaurant, and I was a writer who put on flea markets and rented out the top floor of the church to a karate school and my husband was in film and had long hair and wore headbands, the townsfolk thought we were weird or something. So I did a little survey of things we could do to get us accepted as fellow Amurricans. They included: erecting a flagpole on our front lawn and raising the colors every day — except when the President had a cold, when you were only supposed to hoist it half-way; joining either the local Jaycees, Kiwanis, or Elks — without objecting to the loyalty oath; and swapping our '67 Volvo sedan for an all-American Ford, Chevy, or Dodge pick-up truck — so we could haul around the Little

League baseball team we'd be coaching. We decided to stay subversive.

But probably the biggest con about becoming an ex-New Yorker, particularly after living in Lake County for a while, was the real and ever-present danger of losing the New York Sense of Style and falling headlong into the dreaded Pit of Tastelessness. (The beginnings of this syndrome can be foretold when plastic wine glasses stop looking tacky and start looking sensible.)

The above phobia can, however, be offset by the biggest pro about leaving New York: self-discovery. Living in New York imposes a rigorous set of values and learned responses that many people think are part of them — until they leave. The three operative words in New York are: money, important, and busy. In California, they're more likely to be: fun-filled, self-realized, and karma. When I was in New York, because I couldn't get sufficiently into the operative mode, I thought I was a no-good underachiever, but since I've relocated to California, I've fallen right in with the dominant lifestyle of experimenting with vitamins, getting to know my navel, and reuniting with old friends from my former life in Atlantis.

The dominant mode of transportation outside New York is the automobile. I found it easier to recognize this conveyance when someone explained it was basically the same as a taxicab.

17 SHELTER: From Breadbox in the Sky to Woodbox in the Trees

Adjusting to a whole raft of new information about living space was one of the hardest things about my move from East to West, starting with interior construction materials. In West Marin, they use wood and skip-troweled sheetrock; in New York, steel beams and starched Kleenex.

As in other areas, I had much to learn: my previous conception of passive solar was some sort of wimpy person who hung out in the sun. But one of the things that didn't change much was the outcome of any impromptu remodeling. In New York, the landlord was very likely to send over a representative with a sound background in negotiating—for the Mafia. In West Marin, they don't threaten your health directly, they just promise to bury you alive in paperwork.

Architecture changes names, too. In New York, there are skyrises, brownstones, and tenements. Out here, there's post-Quake, Recent Rustic, and chicken coops.

It came as a pleasant surprise to me that outside of New York, someone didn't have to die before a decent living space became available. On the other hand, only having had experience with apartments, I had to learn a whole new vocabulary about some of the things that come with houses. Below is a list, with definitions:

Gutter: a small metal tray under the eaves in which to collect rotting leaves.

Garbage disposal: a machine designed to eat silverware, after first breaking one's eardrums.

Garage: a place in which to lose cherished household items.

TV antenna: a standing invitation to lightning.

Roof: a scaly, dangerous place one risks one's life to fix.

Landscaping: Nature's way of making sure one has neither any spare time nor money.

Septic system: an underground collection tank for unmentionable wastes that one gets to keep forever, or until it backs up, whichever comes first.

New York is the only place in the country where they celebrate Be Kind to Your Local Baglady Week. What they do is point her towards the nearest garbage can. The closest thing to a baglady in California is a hippie hitchhiker; what we do is point them towards Oregon.

18 SHOPPING: The Bane of West Marin Existence

I remember thinking, as I read Jean Auel's description of the female clan members' hunting and gathering of herbs, berries, and bird's eggs in "The Clan of the Cave Bear," that time hasn't changed very much for the modern hunter-and-gatherer. We can put a man on the moon but we still can't take the *shlep* out of shopping.

In New York, for a fee, one can have the staffs of life—bread and booze—delivered. The rest of the country, and West Marin in particular, seems pretty primitive compared to the ease with which one can gather food and drink in New York. There's very little hunting involved in my hometown, whereas out here, one must scour hill and dale, face clashes with innumerable (gas) monsters or risk getting stuck in a mass herd movement (traffic jam).

As if the hunting and gathering weren't bad enough, there's the paying for to top things off. Californians, being uninitiated into the ecstasy of cut rate, have a disconcerting way of looking blank when one whispers, reverently, the most sacred word in New York: wholesale. And in West Marin, merchants have us over the proverbial pickle barrel; comparison-shopping is a damn good trick when there's only one store.

I can't deny it; I miss shopping in New York. So I'm putting in my request now. Instead of going to heaven or hell when I die, just send my spirit to Bloomie's North.

The East Coast doesn't have an exclusive on pushy, obnoxious-type personalities—they just turn into off-planet flakezoids out here.

19 SMALL TOWN PARANOIA: Why Is That Person Smiling at Me?

One of the carry-overs of being a New Yorker that I've never been able to lose is my paranoia. I wasn't sure I was cut out for life in a small town when it became apparent that my next-door neighbors actually expected to get to know me. Where I come from, neighborliness is the highest breach of etiquette. Lack of same is actually a wise adaptation to the city's living conditions; it's bad enough sharing a bathroom wall with someone you don't know.

But this ingrained attitude did present some problems for me in adjusting to West Marin, where the neighbors often introduce themselves before one has moved in — as well as ask personal questions about one's future building plans. This is comparable to one's next-door neighbor inviting themselves inside one's apartment and then commenting freely on the color scheme in one's kitchen. I mean, just not done! As everyone in New York knows full well, one does *not* give out information about oneself — it could be dangerous to one's lifespan. Ironically, this mind-set will inevitably make country-type neighbors irresistably curious, certain that one has deep, dark and juicy secrets that are well worth the attempt of discovery. And so we move into advanced STP (small town paranoia), the only cure for which is to make up a racy personal history and thus confirm the universal belief that New Yorkers really are a wild and crazy bunch.

Mine is as follows: left in a paper bag on the doorstep of Central Park Zoo, I was raised by the gorillas until I was eight or nine, whereupon I was given my own tire, re-invented the wheel, and split. After making my way arduously to Katmandu, I hung out with llamas and lamas and became a hanger-on among hang-gliderers; the Dalai really dug my act and hired me as a spiritual spy, so I returned to the United States via Papeete, at which time I mothered a child and took up my current occupation: cosmic voyeur.

Since coming to California, I've discovered that when a large enough number of big-city dropouts live together in small towns, they can go from individual to *communal* STP, wherein the whole town shows signs of paranoia. This can result in rabid anti-tourist, no-growth sentiments symptomized by signs ranging from "No spare water, travelers go home," to "Warning! This beach is a hotbed of shark-breeding" to "Swim at your own risk — sea monsters sighted here," to the ultimate in wishful invisibility, small-town vandals who rip up road signs that would direct unwanted traffic to its doors. As a fairly reclusive person myself, I can readily understand this urge to be left alone and hereby confer upon West Marin the Small Towns Prize for Paranoia, good for one group portrait with Art Rogers.

Now if I could just get over this feeling that the walls have ears, the trees have eyes and that somewhere, my house is marked in red on a U-2 photograph....

20 SPEECH:
Whaddya Mean I Tawk Funny?

Due to the rigorous and never-ending efforts of my mother, who was and is a believer in the cause of the King's English, I was never allowed to catch that most heinous form of hoof and mouth disease known as a New York accent. My speech does have a certain nasality, but I escaped the worst of the "dese, dem, and doze" inflections. In my adolescent, wanting-to-fit-in years, this was a cause of despair. I remember my first day of school in a junior high school on the Lower East Side of Manhattan, when a certain Marilyn Berkowitz came up to me after class and said, "Um, me an de udda kids wuz wonderin—how come ya tawk so funny?"

When I left New York, even though I didn't have much of an accent to identify my roots, I did suffer from excessive use of Yiddishisms, which had been part and parcel of my cultural upbringing. Terms like *oy abruch, don't hock my chinick* (a wonderful phrase that translates roughly as "don't break my teacup," i.e., don't bug me), *shmateh,* and *yenta* fell all too trippingly from my tongue, even when my meaning was just as clearly falling on deaf ears. Certain Yiddish words, such as *putz, schmuck,* and *dreck* have gained almost universal acceptance, if not understanding. It was difficult for me to contain myself the first time I heard a Mid-Westerner say, "I schmucked the stuff all the way home."

Speech mannerisms of the inhabitants of my new neighborhood are harder to pin down, most of us being of the less-linguistically-interesting caste of Anglo-Saxons whose major contribution to the language has been a four-letter word beginning with F. Perhaps out of boredom, my mind toys with the West Marin equivalent of certain common New York ethnic phrases, as in:

New York	West Marin
"Meda, meda!"	"Visualize, visualize!"
"Whaddya mean, my mudda? Your mudda!"	"What do you mean your old lady? My old lady!"
"Honky jack-shit bad-ass."	"Narc informer."

| "You want chinks?" | "Would you like to eat some Chinese food?" |
| "So, nu, make me an offer already." | (Unfortunately, no local equivalent.) |

Since the difficult days of my incarceration in junior high, I've learned to appreciate my mother's efforts at keeping my speech relatively pure, even though I did not enjoy, at the time, being accused of having good diction. Now, when I overhear New Yorkers tortuously strangling the language, I have to suppose they've made peace with the fact that only donkeys, geese, and other animals that honk or squawk are their elocutionary equals.

21 STATUS SYMBOLS: Giving Up Gucci

I was never much of a fan of the above designer, mostly because I've always felt that if I wore articles of clothing with someone else's initials emblazoned on them, I should be paid for my services as a mobile advertisement. But that is not the way of most New Yorkers, who, in an effort to distinguish themselves from the hordes around them, line up to pay exorbitant prices for anything that promises to confer Status.

The ultimate status symbol in New York, aside from Vuitton luggage, Cartier watches, and a tan in January, is *space*. This is because there is so precious little of it. The larger one's office or apartment, the greater one's status. But because one doesn't or can't own very much space in New York, New Yorkers end up compensating and owning a lot of little things that take up space, called *things*. Thus status devolves onto the number and quality of things one owns.

When I left New York, after selling my Thonet bentwood, Vasarely prints and Baccarat crystal, I thought I was through forever with living in the land of status-seekers. I applauded California's funky furniture and even funkier clothes as signs that I had finally reached the land of the (status) free. Little did I suspect that only the rules of the game rather than the game itself had changed.

I learned about reverse status, wherein, in redneck country, it's hip to look as dumb as possible by wearing hats made of beer-can labels crocheted together. I learned that people with heavy money often look like free-box *habitues*. I learned that funky vehicles can enhance one's status, providing they're of a particularly cherry make and model. But the one thing that didn't change was the status of *space* — only in California, it takes on the new name of *land*.

Thus, in the land of the Golden Bear, Ultimate Status is conferred by a piece of paper called a *grant deed*. Said piece of paper entitles one to dress as funkily as one wants, drive as broken-down a vehicle as one can get around in, and not even have much of a house. None of the usual requisites of status apply; instead of putting the latest Bill Blass or Ralph Lauren on your back, you merely take the shirt off it and give it to your bank.

Cardio-vascular conditioning—accomplished in New York by running from ne'er-do-wells—is hard to replace in California unless one is a marathon freak, but a popular way to court heart attack in West Marin is by cutting and hauling one's own firewood.

22 STREET SEX: Everybody's Favorite Outdoor Sport

Some of the longest moments in a female New Yorker's life are those spent walking by a construction project. This is because construction workers in the city feel called upon, nay, challenged, to point out the attractions of any passing female's intimate anatomy. "Hey, Joe, see those tits?" "Tits, hell, look at that *ass!*" Indeed, in general, the New York male has quite a proprietary attitude about any female his eyes encounter, letting her know in no uncertain terms if she is pleasing to his visual palate and what, if any, parts of the whole please him most.

By contrast, when I first got to California, I thought I had become invisible. This was particularly true when I lived for a brief stint in the Castro district of San Francisco. Being a woman and pushing a baby stroller in that part of town is a lesson in non-existence. While I didn't miss the jeers and leers of New York, I did long for some sort of neutral territory, in which I wouldn't feel as though my gonads were actually shriveling.

Overall, Northern California wins the non-sexist award hands down over New York; a woman at least has a chance of a nice, hassle-free walk in San Francisco and the odds only go up on the streets of West Marin. My only trouble is, I can't decide whether to think of it as safe or boring. Sexual politics on the streets were played with a vengeance in New York, but at least sex was in the air; out here, due to our somewhat sexual equality and our dairy farms, what's in the air is more likely to be cow manure.

It's platitudinous but true about how time changes one's attitudes; in my flaming feminist days in New York, I bristled like a sea urchin if a man made a pass at me on the street. Now, when I go back East and some importunate male has the gall to comment about my physical person, I smile and say thank you. This is not only due to increased age and perspective; it's also due to compassion. Life can't be a lot of fun for men who have to operate at the pace of, "Hello, how are you, did you come?"

The Marin equivalent of the now-legion harbinger of the graffiti craze, "Taki 183," is "Skids." The issue of defacement aside, one has to admire people who become well known just by virtue of writing one or two words.

23 TOURISTS: Did God Really Create Them, Too?

Pity the poor traveler, trapped in a recreational vehicle with his wife, three kids, dog, and mother-in-law. At least one should *try* to pity him; more often than not, however, the emotion tourists arouse is rage. Where did they learn to drive, I wonder, these tinhorns in tincans — Ma and Pa Kettle's School of How to Drive People Behind You Insane? And why do they *all* come to a dead stop at the corner in front of the Bank of America? Is there an invisible stop sign there or something?

I suspect my dislike of tourists started in New York, where they are considered the lowest form of life. One of the things that prevented me from leaving Manhattan for years was my fear that if and when I returned, I would be mistaken for one of THEM.

It must be cosmic irony at work that seems to land me in places tourists love to visit. Sowing my wild oats in my late teens, I lived in the U.S. Virgin Islands for a time, on St. Thomas. Tourists were the constant thorn in my side, not only offending the eyes with their black socks and Bermuda shorts, but causing numerous auto accidents because of their penchant for driving while under the influence of fermented fruits. They also crawled the roads at a speed reminiscent of snails in a heat wave. An ex-Green Beret friend of mine once suggested mounting a sub-machine gun on the front of one's car, filling it with blanks, and opening warning fire on tourists who didn't pull over when a real person wanted to get by.

My mind has often returned to this image since I've lived in West Marin, where the summers turn the roadways into a modern version of hell, stuck behind cretinous creepers who are oblivious to the fact that the rest of us have things to do, places to go, indeed, unlike the tourist, lives to lead.

I think it's time we campaigned for a one-lane addition to our local roads, the Tourist Lane. All tourists, going in either direction, would be required to use the same lane. This would have a desireable two-fold effect: force tourists to sharpen their wits and driving skills before they left home *and*, in all likelihood, greatly reduce their numbers.

I suppose I should add a proviso here that not all tourists are bad. As Dave Mitchell once pointed out in an editorial in the *Light*, they are a relatively non-polluting industry, from whom many of us make our livings. It's just that they're such fair-weather friends; where are they when we need them, when it's been raining for three months straight and the coffers of the local stores and businesses are running low? But no, they want to come out when it's gorgeous, tying up our roads, stores and restaurants to the point where locals can't get a seat at the Station House on the weekends or bare their privates in private on Shell Beach.

This is going too far and demands affirmative action. From now on, let's all swear on a stack of Jack Mason books that we will not give directions to anyone who wears an I LOVE MY WINNE-BAGO pin.

Of course all of the above pre-supposes that whenever a West Marinite goes anywhere else, she or he will go completely native. This includes driving everywhere like a speed freak, taking the local sights completely for granted, and showing open hostility to anyone who's fortunate enough to be on vacation.

24 WEATHER: You Call This Cold?

As everyone knows, New York's weather goes from the hella-
ciously equatorial in summer — when people walk around in a
"It's-not-the-heat-it's-the-humidity" daze — to the positively polar
in winter, when one's nose, if left out too long, can easily pass for
a Snow Cone.

I thought I could quit the extremes of New York weather by
moving to California but the gods of irony once more had their
fun. My first year out here, living in Lake County, I was treated
to an average summer temperature of 116 degrees. True, it wasn't
humid; it was, in fact, so witheringly hot and moistureless it was
like living in a hairdryer. In the winter, we had snow several times
and a median temperature of 25 degrees, which without insula-
tion is as cold as anything New York can dish up. I had to laugh —
even in New York, we didn't average any worse than the 91
degree difference between summer and winter I experienced in
Lakeport. Actually, I only started laughing after I left Lake
County; while I was there I did a lot of crying.

Then I moved to West Marin, thinking thereby to escape the
worst and enjoy the best of the Northern California climate. Well.
It rained most of my first summer, we had snow on the deck in
winter, and the following year the drought started. Next came
two years of watery deluge, otherwise known as the Flood of '82
and Son of Flood of '82. At about this point I gave up and re-
signed myself to living in a world where changing weather pat-
terns are the norm and normal is un.

When New Yorker friends visit in summer, I get to re-live,
through their eyes, the shock of parched, light-brown hills around
Pt. Reyes. (We call them gold, but who's kidding whom?) Eastern
summers often feel like being locked in a steam bath, but it is also
a season of verdant lushness. If I make the mistake of complaining
about California's drought-or-drown weather pattern, Easterners
always say, "Yeah, but at least it doesn't get cold in the winter."
That's what I used to think, too, until my body's tolerance
changed and it informed me that if subjected to anything colder
than 40 degrees fahrenheit, it was closing up shop and moving to

San Luis Obispo.

My usual riposte is that while the summers are almost a tie, the winters are unquestionably more of a bitch back East, BUT there is at least the compensating factor of fun in the snow. No matter how hard I try to appreciate the milder winter in California, because the rain makes us so house-bound, it's still a time of dangerous over-exposure to one's family. At least there were things to do in the cold in New York; you could ice-skate, ski, or go sledding, and men always had the option of peeing their name into the snow, a really challenging sport since they had to finish before it froze.

Compared to all these snowy memories, I find I just can't get excited at the thought of a mudball fight, and making a mudman sounds dirty, not to mention kinky.

I now stifle my guffaws when anyone, anywhere, complains about the weather. I think it's similar to the Bigger Daddy Syndrome, only for grown-ups: my weather is worse than your weather.

EPILOGUE:
The Last Word

After all the fore-going contrasts between Manhattan and West Marin, I'd like to fantasize out loud about combining the best of both and achieving the divine state of East-West synthesis. If I were in the city, this would entail living at the Dakota, in a penthouse with its own indoor stable. The ideal life in West Marin would be . . . hmmm . . . what I have, plus a hefty inheritance, with the extra-added attraction of a stimulating, non-neurotic literary set. (I said this was fantasy.)

I love New York, in the abstract; I like knowing it's there, that I can stick my finger in its socket whenever I need a jolt. But I love the Tomales Bay Area more than I ever thought it possible to love a hunk of geography. In spite of its foibles—not to mention its Fault—West Marin still seems like a heavenly haven in a stormy world. I can't see myself ever leaving for long and so I have to conclude that, for me, East is least and West is best. Especially if Californians ever get it together and learn how to make real pizza . . .